BENI
and the
BANANAS

Cynthea Gregory

**All profits from this book to go to:
Borneo Orangutan Survival Foundation**

With her debut children's picture book, Cynthea Gregory moves away from her usual genre of writing. Fascinated by the TV series 'Orangutan Jungle School', and troubled by the plight of many creatures whose numbers are rapidly diminishing, she decided to feature a young orangutan as the hero of this book about determination.

When she is not writing she loves to paint, potter in her garden, and discover her environment near and far with her husband.

Copyright © 2023 by Cynthea Gregory

The author / illustrator asserts the moral right to be identified as the author / illustrator of the work. All rights reserved.
No part of this publication may be reproduced, stored in a retrieval system or transmitted in any form or by any means, electronic, mechanical, photocopying, recording or otherwise, without prior consent of the author.

Published 2023 by Mount Hardy Press, England.
Visit the author's website:- www.cynthea-gregory.com

BENI
and the
BANANAS

Beni knows exactly what he wants – BANANAS!
– ripe, soft and yummy.

Beni would eat them 'till he POPPED!

But his Mum said, 'No more, Beni. Too many bananas make you roly-poly.'

'Orangutans need to be able to

RUN,

JUMP,

and LEAP

... through the rainforest to escape danger.'

'Uh-huh,' sulked Beni.

He didn't care about running, jumping and leaping around. His stomach told him he'd rather eat bananas.

While Mum was dozing, Beni sneaked off.

'Bananas here I come!'

While walking through long grass, Beni bumped into an elephant.

'Excuse me, did you see any bananas on your walk?'

'Of course, but I ate them all. Elephants like bananas ya know.'

'Oh no,' said Beni smiling at Elephant. He continued his search, determined.

Beni walked on. At the first banana tree, he started to climb,

'Jackpot, bananas!'

But he hadn't noticed that there was something hidden above him.

Suddenly a ginormous snake raised its head.
'S-s-s-s-cram, I'm trying to sleep,' it hissed.

'I only want some bananas.'
'Go away! My bites are deadly, you know.'
'Oh no!' cried Beni as he slid back down.
The next tree was sure to be better.

'Finding bananas isn't easy,' Beni told himself, 'but I won't give up. They are the best food ever.'

At the next banana tree Beni was more careful, making sure there weren't any snakes. He climbed up and went to snatch his prize.

'Bu-z-z-z-z off you. We live here,' a large bee and his mates flew towards him.
'Go away you pest, we can sting, you know.'
'Oh no!' yelled Beni, really shocked. He had to climb down.

'This is no good, I NEED bananas! I must try harder.'

Struggling through the rainforest, Beni almost bumped into a tiger.

'Hello Tiger, I'm looking for bananas …'
'Bananas! I don't like BANANAS,' roared Tiger,
'but I think YOU'D make a tasty snack.'

'Oh no!' squealed Beni.

Tiger chased him up the nearest tree.

'Hey Tiger, eating me ain't sensible,' smirked Beni, 'I'm full of BANANAS.
Tigers don't eat them you know, 'cos it makes them poo all day!'

'Oh no-o-o-o, rats,' shuddered Tiger, and hurried away.

Beni felt pleased; but still no bananas!

After a long walk, Beni was tired and thirsty. He stopped for a drink at the river.

As he was bending towards the water, two big round eyes were watching him.

Was it a crocodile?

No, something much worse!
A mega KOMODO DRAGON!

The speediest reptile around, who'll eat anything that moves.

'Oh no,' shrieked Beni.

'Get your bum out of here!'

Dragon got closer... and closer... and closer.

Beni ran, but Dragon thundered behind.

'Go Beni go!'

Just when he thought he might be Dragon's dinner, Beni …

... reached a huge mango tree.

'Creatures like you are really yummy,' said Dragon below him.

'I'm only looking for bananas ... but it seems mangoes will have to do,' said Beni, picking a ripe one.

'Would YOU like one?'

'Oh no-o-o-o,' growled Dragon.

But Beni threw the mango at Dragon. Splat! It hit him on the nose. And another.

Splosh! Dragon soon disappeared.

Beni saw it was getting dark.

'Time to go back to Mum — without any bananas.
I'll take a mango back instead, and tell her about my adventures.'

ORANGUTAN FACTS

Orangutan means 'person of the forest'. They are apes which only live on Borneo and Sumatra, in Indonesia. There are between 50,000-65,000 orangutan living in the wild. It is believed that at the current rate of loss, they could be extinct in 50 years.

Orangutans usually live about 40 years. In captivity, they can live up to 60 years. Female orangutans have few babies, as they must look after their young for 6-7 years.

They teach their young how to exist in the rain forest. The fathers do not help at all.

Orangutans eat fruit, bark leaves, insects, flowers and even small mammals (such as birds and rats). When the forest is cut down, they are unable to find enough food to survive.

Orangutans are very clever animals. They share 97% of human DNA. They use sticks and stones as tools to get their food. They will use leaves as 'hats' to keep their heads cool; and as 'gloves' to protect their hands from prickly plants. They also know to eat certain plants if they are not well.

Orangutans eat with their hands and feet They are both used to grip onto trees.

Orangutans make a new nest in the tree tops every night to sleep in. It only takes them about 10 minutes.

Printed in Great Britain
by Amazon